How To Be Happy
No Matter What

Joyce Easterling

Testimonies of how this book has helped are welcome.
You may contact me at:
liveforjoy.easterling@yahoo.com

"A happy heart is good medicine and a cheerful mind works healing, but a broken spirit dries up the bones." – Proverbs 17:22 AMP

"I have told you these things, that My joy and delight may be in you, and that your joy and gladness may be of full measure and complete and overflowing." – John 17:11 AMP

Special thanks to the following for their help and support in completing this work:

The Holy Spirit, for working through me. It is a privilege.

Vincent Jadusingh, for Technical Support. Vince is an outstanding Bible teacher here in Tulsa, and a good friend.

All the members of the Victory Writers' Group, who have critiqued pages and graciously given valuable instruction, as I journeyed down an unfamiliar path to publishing.

Table of Contents

INTRODUCTION

As a young woman, I struggled with depression. Many events, beginning in childhood, perpetuated a feeling of gloom and unworthiness in me that grew roots of depression. It seemed this dark cloud would come over me and as much as I tried, I could not get away from it for days or even weeks at a time. During those times, I often made awful decisions that I later regretted and was forced to suffer the consequences.

Today, I'm glad I suffered those consequences because they helped me begin searching for how to avoid getting to that dark place again. It took some time to be completely free. But it took more than just time and my personal work. It required my surrender to Jesus Christ so the Holy Spirit could guide me on this journey. It was necessary to lay down my pride and work on cultivating my relationship with God. This surrender was the key that started me on my journey and has kept me on the right road- His road to greater happiness through inner joy.

Within the pages of this book, you will find concrete steps you can take to begin finding a deeper level of happiness in your life. If you choose to learn the spiritual lessons from God's word that are presented here your well of joy will grow deeper. You will learn how to live out of that joy each day. Your life will never be the same.

Are you ready for this journey? Together, let us learn what it takes to be truly happy, no matter what.

The Waves

By Joyce Easterling

I saw waves rising over me
Like they would wash over me
And carry me away,
To a place I did not know.

Then I saw dry ground
And stepped onto the path I found,
Never looking back
Until I reached the other side.

My faith has grown strong;
I know now I will never go wrong
Listening to His vision in my heart,
Moving me on to the impossible!

Chapter 1
If the Goal Is To Be Truly Happy, How Do You Define Happiness?

I sat listening to the lady preacher as she talked about how happy her life is and how complete she feels. The joy and peace that was shining from her face as she spoke left no doubt- she truly is a happy woman. The amazing thing about this internationally known teacher/preacher is that she was horribly abused over and over throughout her childhood. Wow! If *she* can be happy, whole, and full of the joy of life, I know I can be too. And so can you, no matter what you have faced. No matter what you are facing today.

So how would you define true happiness? How would the everyday man on the street define true happiness? Part of my research for this book included short interviews with people from various walks of life. You may be surprised to hear how most people define true happiness. Following are a few quotes from men and women around the country who responded to my question.

How would you define true happiness?

"When you are walking in the perfect will of God, and you are debt free and your family is walking with the Lord. This to me is true happiness." – Oklahoma

"Inner peace, which only comes from God." – Florida

"Abiding in the presence of the Holy Spirit; each step directed by Him. He's amazing." –Arkansas

"The ability to be content, fulfilled and satisfied, remaining positive, despite outside circumstances. Happiness is different than joy. Joy to me is only attained through the divine relationship with our Creator." – Missouri

"Having enough money to take care of my family well."
–California

"I think true happiness starts with knowing who you are in Christ and then being content with where you are at in life." –Oklahoma

"True happiness for me is knowing that I am in Gods' perfect will, totally fulfilling His purpose for my life. In that place with God is perfect contentment with great gain." -Tennessee

"Having a strong network of friends, and knowing I'm not alone."- Oklahoma

"Being in good health and at peace with my family."
-Oklahoma

"Happiness for me is doing what I love to do while involving others so they can share in this reality for themselves of love and happiness!" – Florida

"Happiness is an attitude. Has nothing to do with circumstances." –Missouri

"True happiness is knowing God and believing He is always going to make things work out for my good." – Oklahoma

The dictionary definition of happiness uses words like pleasure, satisfaction, contentment, and joy. Notice that natural things like money, material possessions, getting your way, health, love, or sex are not in this definition. The truth is, these natural things cannot create lasting happiness. When most people think of being happy they think of things like- a beautiful day off, promotion, a proposal, a huge raise, and the list goes on. The problem is happiness derived from these kinds of things is fleeting. It lasts only as long as you have that thing in your life. It is a momentary happiness. If you desire to be *truly* happy, you must begin to look beyond the things and events in your life.

True happiness comes from a healthy soul. When your heart contains the joy of the Lord, your soul is healthy. If you belong to Christ joy is in your spirit as part of your spiritual heritage. However, you must cultivate that joy and learn how to bring it into your soul. It's easier to understand this progression when you know the soul is made up of your mind, your will, and your emotions. Your spirit is the part of you that communes with God. His Spirit dwells in you. Therefore you can be happy even though you are alone or hungry. You can be happy while working a job you do not wish to do. You can be happy even when your spouse doesn't love you anymore. You can be happy even though your doctor has said you have cancer. Yes, you really can.

Inner joy produces happiness. True happiness goes beyond your circumstances; therefore it is not dependent upon things going your way. True happiness will carry you through the toughest of times with hope and faith for your future. True happiness brings with it a contentment that makes you strong to carry on until things do get better. (See Nehemiah 8:10.) True happiness helps you see through the pain to the other side and the joy that will be yours then; it will keep you from giving up.

This inner joy that is true happiness is found in the life of God dwelling in your spirit from the new birth. However, you must choose to live out of that joy. This choice happens as you learn to think and live in agreement with God's word- the Bible. It is a process that takes time with the practice of your personal faith.

Life can be pretty tough out there. We need the ability to keep our joy, to remain at peace, with an inner contentment despite all that may be going on around us. In the following chapters, you will find many steps you can take to search for and keep a deeper level of happiness in your life. If you learn the spiritual lessons from God's word that are presented here your well of joy will remain full even in the darkest circumstances of life. True happiness at all the other times in life will just flow!

Chapter 2

Accept the Past So You Can Be Happy In the Present

Anna stood frozen, as she stared into the box she had just pulled from the back of her mom's bedroom closet. Cleaning out her mom's house after she passed on was a dreaded job, but it just became a nightmare. Her legs began to go weak, forcing her to the floor.

Her mind flashed back over the years, half a lifetime, of being angry at her father for the unsettled life he had forced on her and her sisters. Never once was she able to finish a school year at one school, in one town. She had no close friends growing up. Moving every four or five months prevented that kind of normalcy. By eighth grade, Anna felt hopelessly behind the other children in school and believed she could never catch up. So she started staying home from school a lot and eventually dropped out. "It was his fault" she accused.

Memories came rushing in of the many times she begged him not to move them again. "I want friends daddy! I want to get caught up with my class." She replayed his response over and over. "It's not my fault you have no friends. Besides, you have your sisters don't you? They never went to school, and they don't care. You don't worry about school. You don't need it anyway- you're a girl."

The tears began to flow as the reality settled in her mind. "Dad, you were tormented, and we never knew. I hated you for being so hard on us and never letting us settle down. You were so cold and calloused about it; demanding that we just shut up and not question your decisions. You were terrified!" Her heart ached at the thought.

"I was a grown woman with grown children before I was finally able to forgive you, dad. If you would have just told us the truth we could have understood. Even if you told us on your death bed, so many hurtful things could have been healed. Why couldn't you just tell us what happened! It would have put all that pain in its place. So that's why you drank! It wasn't because you was unhappy with us; you were miserable with yourself! All that anger that came out on us when you drank didn't have anything to do with us did it."

Anna's trembling hand cautiously picked up the yellowed newspaper clipping from almost seventy years ago. Sometime over the years it had been carefully preserved by lamination. "Odd," she thought, "that he would want this kept." Then it occurred to her that it may have been her mom who wanted it preserved. "Yes. It would have been like mom to have laminated it, not dad. I wonder if he knew. Maybe she did it always to remind herself what he was capable of when he drank; to keep herself in line. Perhaps she did it thinking they would tell us one day. If so, that day never came."

Anna re-read the headline and caption under the picture of her father as a very young man, "*Statewide Manhunt for Bar Fight Murderer!*" She cautiously read the details of the article, not because she wanted to, but she felt compelled to know it *all* now.

Her father had been in a drunken bar fight and killed a man. Witnesses in the bar knew him because he hung out there regularly after work. They stated he had a reputation for his hot temper. Bitterly, she thought, "Well, that never changed." She continued to read. It went on to say he and his family, a wife and two small children, had disappeared later that night.

Anna's eyes kept returning to the caption where it stated the name of the murderer, her father. She read the name over and over, each time her eyes darting back to the photograph and then back to the name- Robert Jamison. Yes, it was her dad. She had no question about that. He had not changed much over the years. Again, she read the name- Robert Jamison. She reasoned "That explains why mom never had a marriage certificate on the wall, and why my little sisters never had a birth certificate. She said it was a house fire that destroyed those things. That must have been another lie. The last name on those documents was not the last name we all grew up with- Jacobson. He changed his last name! Then spent the next fifteen years of his life on the run, dragging us from city to city, state to state, and living in fear of his past catching up with him. Oh God! Please help me deal with this knowledge. Why didn't they just destroy this newspaper article? I should have never known!"

Your story is most likely different from Anna's. Perhaps as an adult you found out, quite by accident that you were adopted. Maybe your best friend told you she slept with your husband. Your story may be the betrayal of a boss who groomed you for a promotion and then gave it to a less experienced worker you had trained. Have you lost a child? Were you jilted at the marriage alter? Did you have a beloved pastor and friend run off with the church secretary?

Everyone has experienced some emotional pain in their life. These experiences often color or distort our state of mind and present a colossal challenge to forgive. But learn to forgive we must! Otherwise, we stay stuck in our pain, and it festers, poisoning our soul and body. I dare say, to be truly happy while in this state is impossible.

What about the person who has not experienced anything tragic, no real betrayal in his or her life, but still does not feel they are a happy person? The everyday stress of life can build and deplete our joy; especially if we have not learned how to be happy. As you read this book, you will learn some ways we think, speak and act that drain our happiness. You will also learn how to fix these things. Keep them fixed and you will find a greater measure of happiness. I want to emphasize that lasting happiness- that soul joy that carries you through dark times is found in your relationship with God. However, this relationship will not happen just because you are a Christian. We can seek to find principles in the Bible upon which to build healthy practices that will bring the happiness we desire in life.

In looking at Anna's story, we see the results of holding onto the past in hurtful memories, instead of forgiving and letting go of the hurts. Anna was in her mid-fifties when she made the terrible discovery about her father and their family. She had already spent half her life in anger and bitterness toward him. After many years of being a Christian, she came to believe she had forgiven him after he gave his life to Christ. But the regrets remained and the damage to her emotions affected every part of her life. When she discovered the truth, all the anger came back. Now she felt betrayed on top of everything else. Though she was a Christian, her attitude declined. She continued to struggle with how to let God help her deal with her emotions. The questions of 'why' and 'if only' continued to haunt her, bringing further depression to her life. Her thoughts kept her stuck in the past.

This discovery would have never been easy to take. However, if Anna had made the discovery as a joy filled, Christian woman she would have learned to recover as she allowed the Holy Spirit to direct her to forgiveness and hope for the future. The answers she found that put some of her life's puzzle together would have still been painful, but what those answers explained would have brought some comfort to the new understanding. Value would have come from knowing the truth. She would have grown emotionally and spiritually. Instead, she was devastated. We cannot know what is in the heart of another person. But we can see when depression and unhappiness engulf them. If you are that person, please know it does not have to stay that way.

Several years later Anna found the courage to tell her daughter the family secret she had discovered. It broke her daughter's heart to hear the trauma in her mom's voice as she told the story that revealed so many hidden secrets. Anna saw no good in the knowing for herself but felt a great need to tell the truth to *someone*. She trusted her daughter, a happy young woman who possessed a positive attitude in life. Her daughter remembered the scriptures admonition to "cast your care on the Lord, for He cares for you" (I Peter 5:7). She decided to take the hurtful information she learned to God and by doing so came to find comfort in the explanations it brought to some personally painful and puzzling aspects of their family history.

This story demonstrates the drastic difference a happy, positive frame of mind can make in dealing with adverse events that come to our life. Everyone has bad experiences. It is how we respond to these experiences that determine whether they weaken us or make us stronger. What we choose to think about and focus our attention on will create our frame of mind. Our frame of mind colors everything we see, hear, and experience. It also determines how we speak, which will draw positive or negative people and experiences to our life.

The subject of forgiveness will be covered in greater detail in chapter five. In the next chapter, you will discover some specific steps to take that will help increase your level of true happiness. You and I were created to live joyfully. The way to experience true happiness is to learn how to live out of this joy.

Chapter 3

Five Ways to Become a Happier Person

You hear it all the time, "I just want to be happy!" or "If this happened I could be happy". The desire to be happy is the one wish we all share. That hope lies deep in our heart. That is also where the problem lies because many of us have no idea what real happiness is or how to achieve it. So we seek it in places and in ways that cannot produce true happiness. The result is the opposite of our desire. We become unhappy.

Current studies show us that happy people tend to live up to 35% longer and be more successful.[1] A longer, more successful life is a good reason to learn how to be happier. However, the best reason is that true happiness is the product of a joyful soul. We learn from Nehemiah 8:10 that great strength comes from a joyful soul, and that joy comes from the Lord God.

Do you want to learn how to be truly happy? Are you ready to put some work into learning how? If you're shaking your head yes then grab a notebook and a pen so we can get started while you're in the mood.

It is impossible to feel good emotionally while having negative thoughts. One of the most psychologically powerful statements you can speak is "I will." This statement is a decision you are vowing to yourself. These promises you make to yourself hold great power. With that in mind, each step in this chapter will give you a statement declaring your decision to take this step to true happiness. Say the decision statement out loud and then follow the directions in that step to learning how to work it into your life. Determine how you will think from this time forward. In the future, correct yourself when you find your thoughts or words violating the decision you have made.

Step One- Learn how to like yourself.

How we choose to think is a decision on our part. If you allow yourself to think, "I am not a valuable person," you are deciding that you have no value. Your brain will hold the memory of that thought as a decision. If you do not change that decision, the memory of what you believe about yourself will affect your frame of mind, your attitudes, and other decisions.[2]

Unhappy people do not like themselves. Learning how to be happy begins with learning to like yourself. It does not matter what you may have done, what you look like, what you do for a living, or how successful you are- God created you, and He loves you. He believed in you and offered His Son as proof of your value (Psalm 139:14-18; John 3:16). So, as a Christian, the first step in becoming a happier person is to learn to like yourself or like yourself more.

Each of us is uniquely individual, made by God's hand. Psalm 139:14 tells us we are fearfully and wonderfully made. John 3:16 explains God's great love for us in giving His Son, Jesus. That love has never changed. Despite this fact, the Church is full of many people who do not like themselves. Self-worth and being comfortable with "who you are" is basic to being happy.

A young child who is healthy and happy likes himself. The happy four-year-old boy thinks he can do anything he sees daddy doing. Momma's little Princes probably thinks she can do anything too, but mostly, she feels like a Princes. All too often this healthy self-image becomes tarnished and polluted by the words and actions of adults around them. After a few years of elementary school and the harsh realities of teenage years these same children often learn to question themselves and doubt their abilities. They develop low self-esteem and, therefore, lack the confidence to know they *can* have a good life. Disappointment and unhappiness often become a regular way of thinking in adulthood. We can break free from this mentality and learn how to be happy.

The Apostle Paul prayed for the church in Philemon 1:6, "I pray that the fellowship of your faith may become effective through the acknowledge of every good thing which is in you for Christ's sake." Every good thing in you and about you is a gift from God. Take some time now to make a list of all your good qualities. Think about your looks, your personality, talents, things you remember people commenting about over the years, and things that you like about yourself. Please do not move on until you have completed this list. It should be a lengthy list. Ask people close to you to help if you are not coming up with things on your own. You'll thank me later for insisting that you do this. Once you feel the list is complete, read it a few times to make sure you get it- that you have many good qualities. Go back to this list often as a refresher. God loves, in fact, He likes you! Decide- I will like myself.

Step Two- Develop a thankful heart.

Happy people are grateful people. Scripture proclaims the need to give thanks. Psalm 140:13 makes it clear we are expected to be thankful: "Surely the righteous will give thanks to Thy name; the upright will dwell in Thy presence." Thankfulness must be cultivated and practiced on purpose until it becomes your natural way of thinking

You may be asking, "How do I develop a thankful heart?" I'm glad you ask. Take a few minutes now to think about everything in your life you would miss if it went away or had never happened. Take an inventory of everything God had done through you and for you throughout your life. Include your education and other accomplishments. Write down all the marvelous things He has created in the world that you enjoy or would like to enjoy one day. Brainstorm! Include your favorite parts of nature; include incredible things He has given mankind the knowledge to create and you the ability to use. Don't forget to include specific people, past and present who you admire, enjoy, or are simply grateful they exist(ed), even if you never knew them personally. Express your thankfulness to God for these things.

This Thankful List will hopefully be the first of many you will write in your life. This activity can quickly pull you out of the blues and inject a powerful dose of hope into your day. I have developed a habit of writing a Thankful List anytime I find I am feeling down or irritated at life. Thankfulness is a spiritual principle. When you practice this principle, your thoughts and the atmosphere around you become more confident. Developing a thankful heart will help open your spiritual eyes to truths around you that had previously gone unnoticed. Decide- I will practice thankfulness.

Step Three- Learn how to be a giver.

Happy people tend to be givers. They put their focus on others. They are not self-centered in their thinking. Instead, they consider how their actions, words, or silence will affect others, and they adjust accordingly. They may love Saturday afternoons cuddled up with a big pillow watching a movie, but will put that plan aside to volunteer at church or go help a friend who's having a problem. Happy people are willing to give of themselves, their time, and their money or possessions. You will not find a selfish person who is truly happy. Because self-centered people think of themselves first, they don't often help someone else, so they miss the joy the human heart gains when it gives of itself. Develop a giving heart by actively looking for ways to bless people.

Yes, I am going to ask you to make another list. This one will be of everything you could do to give of yourself, your time, your money and possessions. God's attitude toward the giver is, "Give, and it will be given to you; good measure, pressed down, shaken together, running over, they will pour into your lap. For by your standard of measure it will be measured to you in return." (Luke 6:38)

You may have thought this verse was just about giving money, but it is about giving period. Most of your list should be things you can carry out now (not all at once of course). In this list, include a variety of ways to help people. You might consider things like volunteering at church or around the city, supporting a cause, help support a missionary, a college student, a single parent, or a family with a critically sick child. You get the idea. Also, include things you may not yet be equipped to do, but you will be at some point in the future. Ask God to give you inspired ideas on how to be a giver. Be sure to include giving forgiveness to anyone who has offended or hurt you. (I have a whole chapter on the subject of forgiveness later in this book.)

Once you complete this list, go back and highlight the things you can start right away. While it is not possible for one person to do everything, it is possible for every person to do many things in their lifetime. Start regularly giving in whatever ways you choose from this list and grow from there. Decide- I will be a giver.

Step Four- Learn how to become a more positive person.

Happy people are positive thinkers and positive speakers, even when circumstances are negative. If they slip into negative thinking, they quickly pull out of it by looking for and focusing on the good. Positive people live happier lives because more good comes their way as a result of their positive attitude.

I challenge you to look for something good that can come out of even the bad circumstance and verbalize that good. Proverbs 12:14 tells us, "A man will be satisfied with good by the fruit of his words." The Amplified version of Proverbs 18:21 emphasizes this thought, "Death and life are in the power of the tongue, and they who indulge in it shall eat the fruit of it [for death or life]." Begin verbalizing positive thoughts. As you train yourself to do this, your life will change for the better.

Now, I want you to apply Romans 8:28, which assures us God will work things out for our good. Do this by taking a few minutes to think about the most negative/bad circumstance you have had to endure. Briefly write about what happened and how it has affected you. After you have finished writing stop and pray over what you just wrote. Ask God to show you something good that came out of that experience. Now go back over what you wrote and make notes about the things God impresses on your heart in answer to your prayer. You will think of some things that came from that experience that are definite good things. You may think of the words, feel an impression, or see it in your mind like a picture or scene in a movie. Any of these things can be taken as God answering your prayer. Write it down and think about it for a while.

Continue to write any other impression you have or scriptures that come to mind as you work through this step. The goal is for you to learn that even something good can come out of an atrocious circumstance. Perhaps the good thing is something that had not occurred to you until now. Perhaps you were aware of this good thing but did not think of it as coming out of the bad circumstance. This exercise will help you develop a more positive outlook on life. Great strength comes in knowing you can get through whatever comes your way and be better in the end. Remember to give God the glory for getting you through it and helping you see all the good in your life.

We can grow spiritually and personally in tough times. He is beside us every step of the way, ready to help when we ask Him. Completing this step should help you see a more positive side to even your most challenging times. The ability to do this is another key to living a happier life. Decide- I will look for positive things in all circumstances.

Step Five- Give yourself credit for successes.

Give yourself credit for making positive changes in your life. Let me be clear. I am not saying you should think you did it on your own. Apart from Christ we can do nothing with lasting value. Any self-help advice that is void of God's help quickly takes you into pride and deception. However, as you choose to submit to God and trust Him to help you learn from your mistakes and improve yourself, He is pleased and will bless your efforts.

Knowing you have pleased God is something to celebrate! Celebrating your successes is part of loving yourself. We are commanded to love ourselves right along with loving God. "You shall love the Lord your God with all your heart, and with all your soul, and with all your mind (intellect). This is the great (most important, principal) commandment. And a second is like it: You shall love your neighbor as [you do] yourself. These two commandments sum up and upon them depend all the Law and the Prophets." (Matthew 22:37-40 AMP) The implication is we need to love ourselves so we can love other people. If we dislike ourselves, then to love someone else as we love ourselves would be meaningless.

So encourage yourself and regularly consider what progress you've made as you put these five steps into practice. As you make progress on each of these steps write out the things you've learned and the progress you have made. Celebrate your success! Do something nice for yourself. If you do, I promise you will be a happier person, and you will find your happiness positively infecting others. Decide now- I will celebrate my successes.

Endnotes:

[1] http://yourlife.usatoday.com/mind-soul/story/2011-10-31/Happy-You-may-live-35-longer-tracking-sudy-suggests/51016606/1   and http://www.psychologytoday.com/blog/ulterior-motives/201208/happy-people-succeed

[2] *For further reading on this subject see Dr. Caroline Leaf's book* Switch On Your Brain

Chapter 4

Spiritual Laws and Your Happiness

If you are in search of a happier, more joy-filled life, it is important for you to understand about spiritual principles (laws). The dictionary definition of a principle is a fundamental, primary, or general law or truth from which others are derived.

You may be asking, "Why do I need to understand this subject? I want to find out how to find more happiness and joy in my life. What do spiritual laws have to do with that?" The answer is- Everything. Spiritual laws supersede natural laws because spiritual laws are the laws of the kingdom of God. These laws work all the time.

Spiritual laws work for you whether you understand them or not. You will find either more happiness or more problems on your journey based on how you respond to these spiritual laws that govern your existence. If you live your life in a way that violates these laws your life will be negatively affected. Likewise, if you live your life in a way that is in harmony with God's spiritual laws they will change your life in a positive way. A friend of mine had an experience recently that demonstrates this principle.

Vince had just enjoyed a road trip through the southwest and was heading home. He found himself driving through a small country town in Oklahoma, not realizing he had entered a reduced speed zone.

Red lights in the rear view mirror drew Vince's attention. Without hesitating, he pulled over. Being a person of color, flashes of recent news event played through his mind. Fear tried to rise up, but he countered the fear by praying in the spirit.

When the officer walked up to the car, Vince immediately handed him his documents and said, "I apologize for whatever I did." The officer informed him he was clocked going 32 in a 25-speed zone. Vince thought, "What? You pulled me over for that?" However, realizing he was in the wrong he did not say what he was thinking. The officer walked back to his patrol car to take care of business while Vince waited. As he waited, he took authority over the situation by confessing the word of God over it, praying in the natural and in the spirit. As it would happen Vince teaches a bible lesson called "The 16 Spiritual Weapons of the Believer" and was putting into practice what he teaches.

Twenty-five minutes later the officer returned. Because it took so long, Vince figured he would be getting a ticket, but the officer merely gave him a warning. Vince expressed his gratitude to the officer and asked if he could pray for him. The officer said yes. So Vince began to pray over the man's life, his body, his work, and his family.

As he drove out of that little town, God began speaking to Vince's heart. He heard, *Not every divine appointment is going to be warm and fuzzy, like someone prophesying over you or giving you something. Divine appointments can come from bad scenarios. The only way you can turn it around for good is to invite me in. So invite me into all your encounters so I can have my way. Then you will see the divine appointment in the ones that are not so rosy.* Then the Lord showed Vince that the officer needed someone to pray for him because nobody else was doing that right now.

This event would have gone a different way if Vince had acted negatively. He could have been offended by being pulled over for such a small thing. He could have had an attitude. Instead, he took authority over the situation in the spirit, kept his tongue, and cooperated. Then he went the extra mile to step out and pray with the officer. As Vince made his way home that day, he knew he had made a difference in that man's life because he had prayed, instead of getting angry.

Understanding this world has spiritual dimensions allows you to learn many valuable things. Some of those things include: spiritual warfare (II Corinthians 10:3-5), protecting your thought life (Isaiah 26:3; Romans 12:2), and paying attention to the words you speak (Proverbs 18:21). Understanding spiritual laws will help you choose better thoughts and actions, which will affect the quality of your life and your level of true happiness.

In His creation, God set natural and spiritual laws into place. God used spiritual laws to create physical laws, and He did it by the power of faith, which is a spiritual force. I heard Kenneth Copeland explaining the importance of understanding spiritual laws by using the example of an airplane. He explained how the physical world is governed by natural laws that can be used to your advantage. For example, the law of gravity is used to fly an airplane, but that law becomes secondary to the law of lift. Without the law of lift, the plane will not fly. You can fly the aircraft because the law of lift is in operation. However, you must know about the law of gravity to use the law of lift. The law of lift does not take away the law of gravity, but it supersedes it because it is a higher law.

This is how spiritual laws work. If you understand some things about these laws you can use them as the Word of God demonstrates and get the results God intends. Remember, the spiritual world and its laws are more powerful than the physical. Understanding these laws or principles will help you have the best life possible while here on earth.

The spirit world has two functional laws- the law of sin and death, and the law of the Spirit of life. Understanding these two basic spiritual laws will help you to understand the others. Romans 8:2 says, "For the law of the Spirit of life in Christ Jesus has set you free from the law of sin and of death." The law of sin and death was put into operation by Adam when he disobeyed God (see Genesis, Chapter 3). The law of the Spirit of life was put into operation by Jesus Christ at His Resurrection. The law of the Spirit of life supersedes the law of sin and death. Faith is the force that causes it to function in your life.

The Law of the Spirit of Life

The law of the Spirit of life in Christ Jesus takes effect when you accept Jesus as your Savior. This salvation is available to all mankind (Joel 2:32; Romans 10:13). However, all humans do not receive salvation. It comes only to those who put the law of life to work by applying the force of faith. How do we use that faith? With our mouth; by our words (Romans 10:9, 10). Learning to do this is the beginning of the best life possible. The true source of real happiness is found in learning to apply the force of faith to your life. Any strategies you learn concerning how to be happy will always fall short if you do not have this most basic spiritual law activated in your life- the law of the Spirit of life in Christ Jesus.

The Law of Sin and Death

Today, the law of sin and death operates in the world by default because all of mankind do not use their faith to trust in Jesus Christ as their savior. Instead, many reject Jesus, the source of the spirit of life. Even many who have received salvation do not allow the spirit of life to work entirely for them because they mistakenly believe salvation is just to keep them out of hell. They have no real understanding of who they are in Christ Jesus and what kind of life is available to them. Their lack of growing faith blinds them to biblical teachings that reveal our identity in Christ and how to operate in that realm.

The Law of Sowing and Reaping

The next spiritual law I want you to examine with me is reaping and sowing which is sometimes referred to as seedtime and harvest. The law of sowing and reaping is a principle found throughout the Bible. Luke 6:38 say, "Give, and it will be given to you; good measure, pressed down, shaken together, running over, they will pour into your lap. For by your standard of measure it will be measured to you in return." This scripture is a general explanation of sowing and reaping- if you give it will be given back to you. This law covers every part of life: finances; how we treat others; and how we talk. Let's briefly look at each of these areas and how this spiritual law applies.

Sowing and Reaping with our Finances and Goods

II Corinthians 9:6, "He who sows sparingly shall reap sparingly; and he who sows bountifully shall reap bountifully." This scripture is dealing directly with finances, making it simple to see how the law of sowing and reaping works with our money and goods. If you are a stingy person and live your life more as a taker than a giver, you will find your financial blessings to be limited. Of course, other things often affect our income, but financial blessing can take many forms: discounts, rebates, sales, prolonged life of our goods, promotions, etc. Developing a giving heart will cause you to reap great rewards. Those rewards are put into motion by the law of sowing and reaping, mixed with your faith that you will not lack because you give.

Sowing & Reaping by our Action

Galatians 6:7 says, "Do not be deceived, God is not mocked; for what a man sows, this he will also reap." In context with verse 8 we know verse 7 is talking about how we act; how we conduct our life. Jesus' teaching in Luke 6:35-38 goes into great detail about our social behavior and the blessings we receive when we live according to God's directions. I hope you will read this area of scripture in the Amplified Bible for further understanding. (You can find free Bible versions online that are easy to use.) What we sow by our actions toward people comes back to us sooner or later. Selfishness or other questionable behavior may bring you temporary emotional happiness, but will bring much misery later, when your behavior brings unexpected consequences.

Sowing & Reaping with our Words

The power of our words are explained and demonstrated throughout Scripture, but for the sake of space I will show you just a few, and you can study further on your own.

Proverbs 12:14a, "A man will be satisfied with good by the fruit of his words."

Proverbs 18:21, "Death and life are in the power of the tongue."

James 3:2-6 tells us our tongue (our words) determine the direction of our life. Words are a creative force, so this is the power of the law of confession and is part of the principle of sowing and reaping. Therefore, thinking of the word of God and speaking words that agree with Scripture is key to a positive life with *lasting* success.

Many hours could be spent studying each of these spiritual laws. I hope you will spend some personal time studying each one. However, here is a summary of how to live the best, happiest life possible by cooperating with the spiritual laws God has put in place.

Learn to be a giver in life. Speak good things. Refrain from using your tongue to tear down yourself or others. Tell yourself good things will happen in your life. Search the scriptures to find those good things God has promised for His people. Look for His requirements for receiving those good things and learn to do them. Speak the promises of His word over your life.

If you seek to do good things with your life according to God's plan good things will return to you. It is a life-long process as you develop a step at a time. God honors your desire to grow. If you sow good thoughts, good words, and good actions you will reap a reward of good things. The world calls it "what goes around comes around." Yes- it does.

Chapter 5

Like the Breeze (A Story of Forgiveness)

As I sat on the balcony sipping my morning coffee, it seemed like any other day. The cool breeze kissed my cheeks; steam rose from the warm mug, whisking the coolness away. I didn't realize it would be the last peaceful morning spent on this balcony.

It was a lot like life, the steam pushing at the cool breeze, changing it, forcing it to move along. The coffee's steam was pleasant. The breeze was pleasant. But one forced the other to change.

I suppose I was the breeze, and Dave was the steam. He was the stronger personality. Dave always knew what he wanted. He always had a plan. I consistently found myself giving into his plans, even when I felt they were not best. It was my weakness that caused me to mistakenly think that would endear me to his heart. Even after many years of marriage I still felt the need to prove myself to him. In the end, I came to see that I only made myself weak in his eyes.

Later that morning I came inside to wake Dave, and I heard a strange noise coming from the guest bathroom. Dave must be up early, I thought. I headed downstairs to make him coffee. As I passed the bathroom door, I realized the sound I heard was Dave crying. It was the kind of cry I thought you would make if you just heard the news that your child had died. It was a dreadful sound. I broke into the room without even knocking, feeling compelled to run to his aide. I saw him sitting on the edge of the tub with his head leaned down into his hands, his shoulders shaking with each sob. He didn't look up.

"Dave! Honey, what's wrong? What happened?"

Dave slowly looked up at me. His crystal blue eyes were swollen and red, looking more gray than blue. He struggled to find words to answer me, "I-I-ugh." He sighed deeply, "I just had this horrible nightmare. And it felt so real I…it just won't leave my head."

I wondered, what could there be about a dream that would bring this response to an adult man? I laid aside my fears and asked him to tell me about it. So he began.

"Someone told you something I did that they misunderstood. And when I tried to explain you wouldn't believe me." He went on between sobs, "You…you divorced me. And…you found someone else. I couldn't make you understand and…you never believed me." I wrapped my arms around him and reminded him it was just a dream, and now he was awake. I found comforting words to speak, but my heart was troubled. Was he hiding something?

I never made it back to the balcony of that house. The next few weeks I spent longer time each morning reading scriptures and praying. I could not force myself to break away from that special time with the Lord because I sensed a storm was brewing. Something was not right. I had known it for a long time but had been unable or unwilling to face it. Now, as I sat with my

Bible open, I asked the Lord to tell me, to show me the truth I needed to see. I also ask Him to help me help my husband if that was possible. I told my God that whatever I discovered I would lean on His strength to help me through. Let me just say here, never pray a prayer like that if you are not serious, because He will give you the answers you need.

The answers I needed came from Dave himself a couple of months later. We did divorce. What seemed like a terrible ending was a wonderful beginning of a kind of life I had never known and an intimate relationship with Jesus I had previously not thought possible. Dave had made his choices and brought me the freedom I did not know I needed. It has been an awesome journey that has included growth, great victories, and much forgiveness.

Life has become exciting and rich because I decided to ask my heavenly Father the right questions. I asked when I was ready, and He answered. He sent the comforting breeze of the Holy Spirit to fill me with peace, blowing away destructive winds from the raging storm and quenching the fires of anger before they could give birth to hate.

Jesus kept me in His divine arms the whole time as He walked me through the muddy, troubled waters to a higher ground of safety under the shadow of His wings. Through Him, I found forgiveness.

Why You Should Forgive

Do you honestly believe it is important to forgive those who offend or hurt you? Do you consider forgiveness a vital necessity not only for your spiritual life but for your physical health? Matthew 18 records Peter asking Jesus how many times he had to forgive someone and let the offense go. Jesus' answer made it clear that we *always* have to forgive. Then Jesus told a story that He said gave a clear picture of the Kingdom of Heaven. I'm going to paraphrase this out of the Amplified Version, verses 23-35.

There once was a king who wished to settle his accounts with his attendants. As he began going through the accounts, he found one of his attendants was deeply in debt to him for a sum of 10,000 talents, which is almost $10,000,000. The attendant was brought before the king, who was advised the attendant could not pay what he owed. Therefore, the king ordered the attendant, his wife, and children, and all they owned to be sold to pay the debt that he owed to his master.

The attendant fell on his knees, begging him to have patience with him and he would pay everything he owed. His master's heart was moved with compassion, and he released the attendant and his family and forgave him, canceling all the debt he owed.

Later, that same attendant went to a fellow attendant who owed him a sum of 100 denarii, which is about $20, and grabbed him by the throat, demanding that he pay him what was owed. His fellow attendant fell down and begged him earnestly to give him more time, and he would *pay all he owed. But the attendant was unwilling and had his fellow attendant put in prison until he paid the debt.*

When the other attendants saw what happened they were greatly distressed. They went to the king and told him everything that had taken place. The king was angry and called his attendant to him again saying, "You contemptible and wicked attendant! I forgave and canceled all that great debt of yours because you begged me to. Shouldn't you have had pity and mercy on your fellow attendant, as I had pity and mercy on you?" In his wrath, his master turned him over to the torturers in jail until he could pay all that he owed."

Then Jesus made a startling statement. He said, "So also My heavenly Father will deal with every one of you if you do not freely forgive your brother from your heart his offenses."

Notice He did not put any qualifier on the forgiveness. He did not say, "Forgive your brother's offense unless it was a terrible betrayal." There was no "unless" stated in Jesus' teaching.

Being turned over to the torturers, or tormentors as King James puts it, is an awful thing. It carries the idea of physical and emotional pain and vexation. So basically, if we don't forgive we cannot be delivered from all the miseries that arise from our sin. That is an enormous thing! Let's examine this more closely by looking at what forgiveness is and what it is not.

Forgiveness is a conscious decision to let go of resentments, to give up your right to be offended, to purposely stop all thoughts of revenge. Indeed, it goes further than this letting go, which is tough enough. If you are choosing to forgive the person that hurt or offended you, then you cannot secretly hope they will get what's coming to them. Instead, you are to bless them. The best way to fulfill this is to pray for God's blessings to come to them. This prayer is not for material possessions; it is a prayer for God to touch their life with Himself. This genuine forgiveness helps you to focus on positive aspects of your life, and perhaps even of their life. Often, forgiveness will bring compassion for the one who hurt you. It is important to note here that you cannot expect someone else to change or give you an apology.

Forgiveness requires *no action* on the part of the one you are forgiving. Your feelings of anger and bitterness are only hurting you. So forgiveness is actually for you. You cannot be truly happy until you forgive.

Forgiveness is not necessarily forgetting. The memories are a part of you. However, as forgiveness begins its work you can lay aside what happened and not pick it back up. You eventually become able to face that person, even interact with them free of bitterness, resentment, or anger. You can think of that person and not feel emotional pain.

Forgiveness does not mean the offense or hurt was okay. Your forgiveness does not justify their wrong, but it will bring peace to your soul. This peace will help you get past what happened and go on with your life. People who do not forgive are stuck emotionally. They cannot move on. Their personal and spiritual growth is stunted, and they develop an attitude that distorts their outlook on life. This attitude infects every relationship and experience in negative ways.

Remember, it is a process, and you will need the determination to walk in forgiveness. It all starts with saying the words to yourself- in your mind and then out loud. Just saying "I forgive _____ for what he did to me," is very powerful. It doesn't even matter that you don't feel it's true yet. The important thing is that you want it to be true.

The muddy, troubled waters I spoke of earlier was my most challenging experience learning to forgive. It was in this experience that I learned the steps to take so I could truly forgive and stay in forgiveness during the most difficult times. It took time and determination for me to learn how to do the right thing. God always honors that choice.

Like many of you, I know what it is to wallow in anger because of an unjust situation; to feel your gut twist from misery in your soul. I saw my family destroyed, and had years of my life stolen with lies and deception. What I discovered is that thinking about my past that way caused me to focus on all that was wrong in my life. This wrong focus brought deep depression. Un-forgiveness often ushers in depression.

One day I realized I had come to the end of myself and had no place to go but the Word of God because I knew that was the only place I could find healing for my soul. The Holy Spirit ministered to me that I had to pursue forgiveness aggressively. Forgiving him was the last thing my flesh wanted to do. It wasn't fair. But my spirit knew that was the only way to recover. One of the greatest admissions you can make to God is *I do not want to forgive, but I am willing to allow the Holy Spirit to help me become willing.*

Joy cannot live in a heart filled with resentment and bitterness because happiness and un-forgiveness are opposites. If you begin digging out the un-forgiveness, there will be room for joy to come inside. For me, this took some time and much effort. I knew from scripture forgiveness was not an option. In my quest to learn how to forgive him I searched the scriptures regularly for every hint of help offered. I always came out of my studies knowing God would help me. I wanted my happiness back. I wanted to feel joy in my heart again. I had to learn how to forgive him.

I want you to see the process I went through in coming to forgiveness in this situation. The process is the same for any event you come to in life that requires your forgiveness. First, admit you have not forgiven, and then confess it as sin. State your desire to forgive and ask God to help you. Then pray for the one you need to forgive. Ask God to bless him or her anytime you remember what happened. If possible, find a way to be kind to them as an act of forgiveness.

I remember the day I began telling God, "I want to forgive him. I know you require it, so I want to obey. My desire is to move on from this thing and be stronger." Eventually, I was able to add, "I want him free from my wrath hanging over him. That is doing neither of us any good. Father, help me to forgive him. I cannot do this on my own!" He heard me.

My heart was impressed to begin praying for him to be blessed anytime he came to mind. This was an extreme request, so I made the extreme effort and started to pray for him to be blessed. Each time something would bring a dark memory from our past to my mind I would earnestly pray for him. Soon I found that when we had to talk or get together because of our children I could be kind. The day came that I could easily remember the good things about him and good times we had without the dark things shadowing my memories. I even began to feel compassion rise in me that desired healing for his soul. This changed everything for me.

Forgiving my ex-husband brought me to a place of realizing my failures in our marriage. God ministered to me that what happened was not my fault, but I did contribute to problems in the relationship. He helped me face those through the Word. Over time, this brought healing to my soul. The thing I had been praying for my ex-husband came to me. God is so good, always working in every situation we encounter.

If you find yourself angry when you think of a person or remember a situation talk to God. Tell Him you are sorry for not forgiving this person. Ask Him to forgive you and to help you forgive them. Make the commitment to change how you allow yourself to think about him or her. Then say a prayer for the one who hurt you. Ask God to help them deal with their pain and to bless them by making Himself real to them.

Next, you must move on from the event in your mind. Accomplish this by no longer seeing yourself as a victim. Take back the power you gave to them by feeling victimized. Take steps to see how unforgiveness has affected your life, health, and relationships. Realizing this will help you to not pick up the pain again. When the hurtful thoughts come to your mind, immediately tell yourself, "No. That is done. I have dealt with that. I have forgiven, and I am forgiven." Then move on to a healthier vein of thought.

When you choose to let go of offenses and grudges, your life will begin to change for the better. But don't think this is a one-time thing. Some hurts are so deep this process must be worked through many times. Trust me, if you keep forgiving, you will keep growing past the pain and the day will come when you find you are free.

Now let's take a quick look at the other side of forgiveness. Perhaps you are the one who needs forgiveness. Start by going to God in prayer to repent of your actions or words that hurt or offended someone. Accept in your heart that He will forgive when you ask. Then, if the person you hurt is alive consider asking them for forgiveness. They may not give it, but it is the asking that helps further your healing. Even if they do not give forgiveness immediately, they may later as God works on their heart.

Remember, you do not forgive someone because they deserve it. Obedience to God is always the right choice for our life. When we disobey, a wall of guilt is put up between God and ourselves. This wall causes our spiritual and emotional strength to weaken because it blocks our peace and joy. Unforgiveness is the thing most often used by Satan because he knows it separates and divides relationships and hinders our fellowship with God.

The poison of unforgiveness in the soul creates infections of bitterness, resentment, anger, and hatred. Just as poisons and severe infection in the body will bring death if it is not removed, so the poison caused by harboring these bad feelings will bring spiritual death if not rooted out and replaced by forgiveness.

Forgiveness is often called a miracle medicine because it brings great healing to the soul, which brings healing to the body. It is simple to find many writings on the psychological and physical health benefits of forgiveness. An internet search will pull a list of these articles relating a healthier, longer life to those who are quick to forgive and ask forgiveness. Studies in recent years by leading medical scientists have proven the connection between unforgiveness and a long list of health problems. Of course, this does not automatically mean if you have one of these illnesses you have not forgiven someone. Each of these issues can have many causes. However, there is now verifiable evidence showing unforgiveness is a factor that can lead the way for many illnesses of body and mind.[3]

Forgiveness begins with how you think; how you think about what someone did to you or said about you and how you think about that person. Thoughts create our attitudes, and they come out in our words and actions. The torment in our soul displays itself through how we talk and act. So stop the thoughts as soon as you start to think them. Immediately, not in a minute or two but immediately stop the thought. A minute or two will probably be too late because you will be sliding into an emotional pit by then. The Apostle Paul taught us in II Corinthians 2:10-11 that if we forgive Satan will not have an advantage over us. I think that sounds like an excellent thing- to keep Satan from having an advantage over my life.

If you stop thinking about the offense, you will stop talking about it. In other words you drop it, let it go, which is exactly how the Amplified translation of the Bible defines forgiveness in Mark 11:25...let it drop (leave it, let it go). I dare to say that the power promised us in Mark 11:23, 24 depends upon how well we obey verse 25. To forgive is love in action. Galatians 5:6 tells us faith works by love. So when you love by forgiving your faith is energized!

When you obey God by acting out the principle of forgiveness your emotions will calm down and healing will begin. Happiness will find its way into your heart again. I have found this to be true in my life. So I forgive and in doing so I choose to be happy. Will you do the same?

Footnote:

[3]To read further see: http://www.mayoclinic.org/healthy-living/adult-health/in-depth/forgiveness/art-20047692

Chapter 6

True Happiness Cancels Out Lonely

I find it amazing how we can be in a room full of people and yet feel alone, or be in a marriage and feel lonely. I married with overwhelming feelings of loneliness. I mistakenly thought being married would clear that up. It's true that while we dated I was distracted from my loneliness by the emotions of love and lust and my fascination with this young man. I was only seventeen back then, but I have observed the same phenomenon in middle-aged adults who have never learned how to be alone.

It is very interesting to me that out of the Ten Commandments from the Old Testament the first four are about our relationship with God. The last six commandments are about our relationships with other people. Let's look at Matthew 22:35-40 in the NAS version. The religious leaders of the day ask Jesus which of the commandments is the greatest. Jesus replied, "You shall love the Lord your God with all your heart, and with all your soul, and with all your mind. This is the great and foremost commandment." This references the first four commandments. Jesus continued, "The second is like it, 'You shall love your neighbor as yourself.' On these two commandments depends the whole Law and the Prophets," referencing the last six commandments. The clear message here is it is all about the relationship- first to God, then to other people.

Real loneliness is an emptiness of the soul. Although we sometimes say we feel lonely when what we desire is companionship or fellowship, this is not real loneliness. The need for friendship will cause feelings of isolation that we interpret as loneliness, but finding a group or two to get involved with will usually take care of that need. However, real loneliness deep inside comes from a spiritual sickness. God uses the feelings of loneliness to draw our attention and get us to look to Him. The only way to satisfy real loneliness is through an active, intimate relationship with God. That is not to say that a Christian cannot be lonely, but if we are it is a simple fix. Begin spending more time with God in His word.

The Word (the Bible) is medicine to our soul. As we read and pray, we can listen in our spirit for Him talking to our heart. I often write these conversations down in my journal and reread them from time to time. As we engage ourselves in this daily fellowship with God, we find a fullness of joy entering our soul that clears away any trace of loneliness lurking in the background.

Why would a Christian not be actively pursuing this type of relationship? Often it is because of distractions in daily life and forgetting to set our relationship with God to be the number one priority. Time with God in His Word has to come first; first in life and first in your day. Spending just 10 or 15 minutes each morning reading some scriptures with prayer and listening for Him to speak will set the day off to a better start.

Remember, prayer is a conversation with God. Conversation is two-way. Don't be concerned about any formality or if the words are right. I read a quote from Lloyd John Ogilvie in his book, *The Greatest Counselor in the World,* "The Holy Spirit takes our mumbling, disjointed, mixed-up words, so often jumbled in with our own selfish desires, and edits the whole thing." Years ago I started with a few minutes each morning. It has grown over the years so that I get up quite early each morning just to have more time for devotions. My day, my life requires it, and the devotion fulfills me.

This spiritual activity of reading scripture, prayer and listening each morning helps us learn to practice His presence throughout the day. As we are at work or play, we will find the Holy Spirit reminding us of things He has told us in our devotion time. I sometimes have the Holy Spirit speak something, a valuable lesson or point, in my heart as I watch a movie or type on my computer at work. God desires an active relationship with us. He is eager for our fellowship and delights in bringing answers to our requests. Our heavenly Father is the very best of Fathers. He is loving, kind, giving, merciful, full of wisdom, and very generous. This relationship fills our soul with joy. A soul that is full of the joy of the Lord is truly happy and finds no space for loneliness.

Chapter 7

Attitude Is Everything!

Jerry was an easy going man who always loved to joke and laugh. He had the best laugh. You could see it in his eyes: he was a happy man. The incredible thing about Jerry's attitude is that the facts of his life did not always support this joyful personality. He spent many years in poverty.

Throughout Jerry's twenties, he worked menial jobs at deplorable pay. He had not finished school, so jobs were limited for this country boy. He became a gravedigger and janitor for a mortuary in his early twenties and later dug ditches for the county. Eventually, he worked as a gofer for a small group of building contractors. Jerry gave very job he took his best effort with a happy, hopeful attitude. He intended to be his own boss someday and knew that was going to take much effort. He figured with hard work and God's help he would eventually fulfill that dream.

The birth of his first child came with much emotional trauma. There were complications due to the doctor's negligence. Mother and baby almost died. The baby's injuries gave the first month of her life great physical pain and almost unbearable emotional pain to Jerry and his wife, Susan. Through each trying day, Jerry could be found singing and humming as he worked. He looked forward to being home each evening to help his wife and spend precious time with their little daughter. He enjoyed talking to the baby and Susan about how beautiful they both were and how this time would soon be past and life would be grand.

The pregnancy and other genetic issues, along with the traumatic birth adversely affected Susan. She became nervous and agitated with deep bouts of depression. Susan remained in this state for many years and through another pregnancy that almost took her over the edge emotionally. Through it all Jerry remained steady as a rock. His joyful personality and hopeful attitude were an anchor for Susan. Eventually, she found much peace and growth in a newfound relationship with God and began to allow her husband's outlook on life to affect her more positively.

Eventually, Jerry did become a small business owner. He founded a small service business after many years of hard work in the field as an employee of many difficult business owners. The business grew past each hurdle. Jerry became known as an honest, hard-working man who was pleasant to deal with and did the job right.

After ten years in his business, Jerry suffered a major heart attack and had to receive several by-passes. The doctors said he could no longer work. The Rheumatic fever he had as a child had severely damaged his heart and years of hard work had stressed it beyond the limit.

At age 42 Jerry found himself disabled and without a way to support his wife. Susan had to take a job for the first time in her married life. Jerry was heartbroken to be forced to send his wife out to work each day while he stayed behind. Many mornings he sat in his recliner with tears streaming down his face as he prayed for strength to be given to Susan in her new position as the breadwinner. Even the thought of her burden was painful to bear.

Incredibly, Jerry kept a pleasant, cheerful attitude through it all. He found things to make his life happy and fulfilled. He learned how to keep house and, much to his surprise, how to cook. Each morning he walked the mall with friends he had made on his morning rounds. Eventually, he began helping clean and repair small things at church. He even found a creative outlet by developing a woodworking hobby. Growing up in the country Jerry always enjoyed birds, so he began to study them and became an avid bird watcher. He even came to love reading- mostly westerns.

I think the most powerful change he made was spending a lot of time in prayer and reading the Bible. It was this activity that kept him motivated to continue in the others. Eventually, he found fulfillment and purpose in serving as a deacon in their church. When Susan came home from her job, Jerry would sit on the floor in front of her and massage her feet, telling her how much he appreciated her. Then he would serve her dinner and clean up afterward. Jerry resolved he would enjoy his new life, despite missing his previous career.

Jerry retained his refreshing sense of humor, keeping him at the center of large family gatherings as he told stories and jokes keeping in-laws and cousins laughing and asking for more. Through the next 23 years, doctors frequently told him they could not figure out why he was still alive. Because of the condition of his heart at the time of his by-passes the doctors did not expect him to live another ten years. (Of course, they did not tell him that at the time.) As the years went on each test showed damage to his heart, yet he carried on with strength. Doctors were astounded to hear that he was daily walking the mall and cleaning house. At one point, his specialist told him, "Jerry, I don't know how you can do all you are doing, but I can tell you don't ever stop. *You are a miracle.*"

At age 66 Jerry died. He had become ill and developed congestive heart failure. As we read the journals he had written through all those years, it is obvious he remained a genuinely happy man. His deep love of God and appreciation for the little things in life shown through right to the end. People can hide a lot. My dad, Jerry, was not faking his joy for life. In fact, the doctors say it added 24 years of life he would not have had without his wonderful attitude (and the walking helped).

Our ability to maintain a healthy attitude no matter what circumstances come is a key to living a happy life. When our attention remains focused on our relationship with God, a joyful attitude will result. This attitude will positively affect all our relationships, producing a higher quality life.

Chapter 8

Healing and Your Happiness

Can you be truly happy when you are sick? Yes. You can if you know Jesus is your healer. And you can if you are at peace about where you will spend eternity. It's a little bit like choosing between two of the most pleasant vacations you could ever dream of taking, knowing you will never have to return to your ordinary life. Every time you receive healing, you are changed forever by your faith becoming stronger. On the other hand, if you go to be with Jesus, well, what is there to be sad about that!

I cannot say I walk in perfect health. Honestly, I do not personally know anyone who claims that; although I fully believe it is possible. I have had many healings in my life. Some were minor ailments and some were bigger things. You can be sure that all of them were important to me and helped my faith on down the line. Sometimes it did frustrate me though; to know I had received healing for a couple big things in my life, so why can't I quickly shake this cold or arthritis? As I studied deeper into what the Bible has to say about healing and how to obtain God's best for my life I began to realize something. Like it or not I have a role to play in whether I receive the full healing God has provided for me. Now, I cannot tell you why some things seem easier than others. I have read about people that had a miraculous turn around in a cancer diagnosis and lived their days out but continued to struggle with the everyday things like colds and such. Does that make sense to me? No.

I have to say that other things do not make sense to my mind. For example, we recently lost a well-loved pastor in this town. This man had compassion and humility flowing out of him. I could feel it so strong when I would shake his hand. In years of attending many of his services, I can say that I never left one without knowing I had heard from God and took something away that helped me. He died in his early 50's of cancer. It makes no sense. We must leave these things to God and not lose our faith in questions we cannot yet answer.

We cannot see everything as God can so we cannot understand such events. These things happening do not change what God has done and what He has provided through Jesus. We all have an allotted time, and none of us knows when our time will be over. I choose to believe that I will live a long full life, whatever long is for me. I also choose to believe the teachings of Christ and what He has done for us. I will take everything I can get of what He has for me. The scriptures clearly show the blood of Jesus paid for our healing the same as for our salvation. So for me, that is a settled fact. When I miss something, I will endeavour to move on and try again because I know the fault is not with God.

Operating in this attitude is part of living in faith. This attitude will help keep your joy full during these trials. Doubts and questions about why drain away joy and will prevent you from moving forward to the happy, abundant life God has for you now while on this earth. Questioning God and doubting the truth of His Word because of your circumstances will weaken your faith and usher in a depression.

I want to give you a personal testimony that happened when I was much younger spiritually and in years. It demonstrates some of the principles I have been talking to you about, even though I was just learning to walk in faith at the time.

When I was in my twenties and early thirties I suffered from migraine headaches. When they would come, they would be debilitating. I would have to lie flat on my back because any movement made my head feel like it would explode. Misery was compounded by vomiting that always came with these headaches. It would last about twenty-four hours and then slowly taper off on the second and third day. My life, my job and taking care of my family came to a halt while I recovered from these migraines. The medicine prescribed did not work for me- nothing worked. I prayed desperately, crying to God for them to stop. I saw in His word that He had healing for us, and I had experienced that in other areas; but this thing would grip my life, and it seemed I had to just ride it out.

I had been attending Bible School at our church. We were in the middle of a course by Kenneth Hagin Senior on healing. Also, some of Kenneth Copeland's teachings were a part of that course. I began spending a lot of time studying intensely about healing in the Word. I dedicated myself to it. I read the Bible, I read books from every Christian author I could find in our church library. One of the principles that stood out to me as I studied was that faith receives God's peace while in the situation, and the joy of the Lord will give strength to endure until your answer manifests.

Several months after I completed this study one of these headaches came on strong. Almost a year had gone by without a migraine, so I was very disappointed that it returned. It hit me on a Sunday afternoon. A Christian praise band I enjoyed was giving a concert at church that night. I had looked forward to this event for weeks. A consistent theme in my studies on healing was the importance of praise and worship to God even if I did not feel like praising at the moment.

According to the past, this migraine meant I would miss the service and spend the night on my back between bouts of throwing up. This time I became angry at the devil for trying to steal my health and my enjoyment of this praise service. I recognized God had something special for me to receive that night, and I was not going to give it up. So I decided I would stand my ground against the enemy's attack. I told my husband I would be going to the service and if I had to step out to the restroom to throw up, I would. I did go that night. All through the service I kept my mental focus on the healing that Jesus had provided for me. As I paid attention to the words of the songs the band sang, I praised God in my mind for all He has provided and for being my God.

Understand, the whole time I was doing this I felt my head would explode any minute unless I passed out first. I did have to step out a couple of times. I admit the whole evening was not enjoyable. But I was doing battle, and it felt like it. I refused to give up!

About 30 minutes before the service was scheduled to end I excused myself to go to the car. I told my husband to stay for the length of the service- I would be praying outside. I lay reclined in the seat of our car for the next half hour while I continued to pray- sometimes in the spirit, sometimes with my understanding. I kept thanking God for healing, for *my* healing that Jesus provided by those stripes He took for me (I Peter 2:24). I thanked Him for cleansing me of what was causing these headaches. I thanked Him for being such a good God.

I was praying out loud now. I remember telling God that I fully expected this pain to go away and never return. I began to practice what I had been studying. I said, "Satan, you take your hand off me because I am God's property, and sickness does not belong on God's property!" I did this in the name of Jesus and spoke the power of His blood over my life. I recall asking God if I had any sin I was unaware of that might be causing unconscious guilt. Nothing came to mind. (Of course, now I know that Jesus' blood covered my sins and the migraines had nothing to do with unconfessed sin. It was Satan doing his best to take me out and derail me from God's purpose for my life. However, I prayed in the level of maturity I had at the time.) I continued praying. I did this out loud, but it was only a loud whisper. That's all I could do without adding intense pain. I was forcing myself to concentrate on what I knew the scriptures say about healing instead of the pain I was feeling. I knew it was a migraine, but it was also an attack. So instead of going to bed and thinking how upset I was I went after my healing.

Suddenly, I felt a very powerful unction down inside. I recognized this as the voice of the Holy Spirit directing me, but what I heard astounded me. It was simply, "Sing." I stopped praying and told God, "Sing? Are you kidding? Just talking out loud is vibrating my head to the point that I'm feeling dizzy, and I honestly feel like it is going to break open. Now you're telling me to add to that pressure by singing? How can I sing? Just talking out loud is taking my breath?"

Finally, people started coming out of the church and thankfully my family was in the first wave, so we were able to exit the parking lot quickly. Dave looked over at me and asked how I was doing. I replied, "I feel like I've felt for the last several hours, but I am the healed of God, and it will manifest for me tonight. Then I will never have this pain again." He replied, "Hallelujah, I believe for that with you!" While he was saying this, I heard it again, that unction down inside saying, "Sing." So I told Dave what was happening and that I was going to obey. I think I also added something like, "don't think I'm crazy, but I have to do this".

So I began to sing. I sang a worship song as loud as I could, which was not very. But God appreciated the effort because instead of my head getting worse it was very slightly better. About two miles from the church my husband and two children began singing too. We lived about twenty minutes from the church, and we sang all the way home! Somewhere between half way and home my pain stopped. By the time we reached the house, I was fully recovered. That was almost thirty years ago.

I have never had one of those headaches since! Have I had bad headaches? Yes, but nothing even remotely like a migraine- ever. There have been times a sinus headache would start to feel like a migraine trying to come. I have been quick to remind the enemy of my soul, "No you don't! Jesus has healed me of that, and you are not allowed to lay it back on me. Be gone, in the name of Jesus." And it would go. Sometimes it would become a low-level sinus headache that was just annoying, but most of the time it would go away entirely. Even these headaches have been rare in the years since this healing. If God did this for me, He would do it for you too. Don't allow your spiritual enemy or your pride tell you it is foolish to deal with sickness this way. It is, in fact, the first line of attack you should take against whatever afflicts you.

Satan oppresses people with sickness, and Jesus heals people who are sick (Acts 10:38, I Peter 5:8). God desires an abundant life for you, and the devil wants to steal, kill and destroy (John 10:10, Romans 5:17). If you are sick, God wants you well. He created your body to function according to His design. If you think God wants you sick you are mistaken. However, you have a part to play in your health and wellness. If you believe that your only part is to ask and believe, but then go on living, eating, thinking, and speaking the same old unhealthy ways you always have you are mistaken. I recommend that you kick the devil in the pants and begin renewing your mind with God's word in the area of healing and all that affects your health. Study what God thinks about your thought life and the words you speak. Make this a mission of love for yourself to develop and grow- to prosper in your soul and your body. Victory is yours to walk in, but it is not automatic. Claim your victory and begin to learn how to walk in healing and wellness. It is important to not allow yourself to feel condemned when you are sick. Condemnation is a trick of the enemy to bring discouragement, thereby weakening your faith.

This healing built my faith and inspired me to continue with my study of healing. I revisit this study at least once a year and often several times a year, refreshing my spirit and renewing my mind with truths from God's word on healing. I often talk about God's grace to heal and endeavour to find keys in the scriptures on how to receive and maintain healing. I knew faith in the truth of God's Word was a key, but I also knew there was more. Otherwise, we would not have to continue to battle with this defeated enemy.

Jesus dealt with disease in Jesus' death, burial, and resurrection. He has provided for our healing and wholeness (Isaiah 53:4-6; I Peter 2:24). However, it is not automatic. We have to receive it and stand firm, even in the face of pain or a diagnosis. There is always a standing time between the start of the symptoms and the disappearance of all symptoms. What you do during that standing time has everything to do with how you receive and keep your healing. We have to learn how to be strong and carry on in faith toward God even if the healing doesn't come in the time frame we desire. A healthy attitude in that situation says, I

know I don't understand everything, but G
and He is still in control."

A positive, happy Christian is in the best position to receive their completed healing. I am grateful for doctors and medicine. I believe it is God that has given these gifts to mankind. When I pray and stand for a miraculous healing, I will not beat myself up if I don't receive healing the way I wanted it. I will take it any way God can get it to me. But I am challenged more and more always to seek Him in prayer for healing first and then give myself a time of standing, waiting and praising Him for the healing I know He is bringing. It's okay if I end up having to go to a doctor. I thank God that I can go and get what I need. Then I begin talking to God about how to move into divine healing when the next thing comes.

I have had divine healings and medical cures. I am thankful for them all. However, I want the divine ones most of all because they bring God more glory and are a greater blessing to my life. Either way, I refuse to lose my joy. I am determined to be a happy person and live out of the joy the Lord has put in my heart. I pray you will make this same decision today.

Chapter 9
Happiness No Matter What

In May of 2012, I was diagnosed with lung cancer. The circumstances that lead to this cancer being found were a divine act of grace and mercy. In retrospect I realize I had not been well for a very long time. However, I did not realize that my growing fatigue and susceptibility to viruses and other sicknesses going around had anything to do with really being sick. I would pray and speak scriptures over myself and much of the time would feel better quickly. However, the susceptibility remained, and sickness would return over and over. I knew I did not eat as well as I should, and regular exercise was not part of my routine because of my lack of energy and joint aches. So I believed I was causing it by not being disciplined enough. I struggled greatly with this, and the guilt of it weakened my faith. Like many of you, I subconsciously thought I had to be good enough to receive healing.

I had been lead to study healing, faith and confessing God's Word for years. So I regularly confessed Jesus as my healer and spoke scriptures over my life. When doubts would try to come in the form of questions- What am I doing wrong? Do I have unconfessed sin? Am I not believing enough? Am I being punished? I would go back to the Word and the healing message I found there rang strong in me from Isaiah 54 and other scriptures. I knew healing was real;

it was provided almost 2,000 years ago through Jesus. So I claimed it as mine.

This journey began one Saturday in February of 2012 when I developed an earache. It was my Eustachian tube, and it grew worse through the week, with the pain going into my jaw, neck and down my back. On Monday, I went to my doctor who confirmed that sinus drainage was causing a blockage in the Eustachian tube, and she gave me a new medication. The second day I took this medicine I ended up at urgent care with a severe allergic reaction. The next week when I visited my regular doctor for a follow-up on this event she asked how my ear was doing. I had started taking over the counter allergy medication a few days earlier, so I advised her that my ear was fine, but my back still hurt. It felt a bit different than it had before when my ear and jaw was hurting too, but the nagging backache was still happening.

My doctor immediately grew somber and said she did not recall me mentioning my back. I did not remember if I had told her my back hurt or not because it was minor compared to the ear and jaw pain. She said with my family history the jaw and back pain may have been my heart, so she would have to get a chest x-ray. Two days later her nurse called to say the x-ray showed an abnormality and the doctor had ordered a CT of my chest. I assumed the abnormality was in my heart, but the nurse did not explain.

Two weeks later when I went back to get the CT results she informed me the CT revealed a mass on my right lung. The location of the mass was in one of the primary bronchi going into the lung. The best course of action recommended was a pet scan because it would reveal if the mass were neoplasms. She made sure I understood that because of the location of the mass, it would have to be removed even if it were not active cancer.

The next week I had a pet scan that revealed the mass was neoplasms. The next step was a lung biopsy to see if the mass was actively growing. They believed it was and gave me medical reasons why they thought it was growing. The biopsy confirmed it was cancer, a Carcinoma, and it was very active. I was scheduled to have surgery three weeks later. Many details at home and work had to be organized since I would be in recovery for almost two months. The doctors informed me it was a very complicated surgery, but I had been scheduled with one of the top thoracic surgeons in the state.

Two months passed from the day I heard my original CT results until the date I had surgery. I knew all the years of studying healing had prepared me for this time, and I would reap the fruit of faith. God's strength was strong in me, and I can honestly say fear did not grip my heart. I remember thinking several times about the natural possibilities of such a complicated surgery- I knew there was a real possibility of dying, and this knowledge tried to bring fear. But I also knew there was nothing in me that made me think I was going to die. I knew God was with me and had a plan for my life that required my being here! I had decided I would accept healing however God could get it to me. This was my attitude when I spoke to people who ask how I was doing while I waited for the surgery day. I knew I would be okay. I also knew that if I did die I would be with Jesus, and that would be an awesome thing. However, I believed I would be fine and would have a strong testimony when it was finished.

Between the time the mass was first discovered and the surgery date I was asking God to bring healing before I had to go into surgery. I did not want to go through the pain and all the weeks of recovery. Also, I did not wish to be off work all those weeks. Despite that, I did have to go through it all, but I felt God's strength and presence the whole time. It never seemed too hard. I never felt afraid or angry, but only grateful and peaceful that I was in God's hands. This was purely the work of the Holy Spirit- that peace that passes all understanding. This peace was evidence of His grace upon me; to walk through this time with the thought to use the experience as a tool to help others in the future. My heart remained joyful even as I walked through the physical sickness. I can honestly say I remained a happy person even while I waited to see the outcome.

You see, I believe God heals in different ways. Sometimes instantly, sometimes gradual as we commune with Him in His Word and prayer while learning to put it into practice. Other times He works through the hands of doctors and the use of medicine. Never doubt that it is God who has given us, in His grace and mercy, men and women who have the talent and drive to doctor mankind and develop better methods for bringing healing through medicine. This is another way God heals us. Although we may not understand why we have to walk through some situations, we can be sure He is walking with us and directing those who are bringing us help (see Psalm 118:7). All the glory goes to Him! We can be confident that He always wants us well and has provided for our healing. However, we do not always understand what hinders us. Even in those times we can rest assured He is with us and He is for us. He will minister His healing to us by any method we can receive.

I want to share with you an experience I had the night before my surgery. I was lying in bed thinking about going into this major surgery the next morning. The natural possibilities were starting to run through my mind- What if I'm wrong and I die? What would that experience feel like? What if something goes wrong and I'm left in a coma? How would my children and grandson handle that event? I remember telling the Lord, "I know these are just natural thoughts, and I refuse to pick up any of them. They have no part in me because I know I am not going to die, and I will be okay. You have healing and health for me. I have confidence that you have not brought me through everything I've gone through in my life for it to end now, with my purpose undone.

I began praising Him in my mind and whispered breaths as I lay on my bed. Then the thought returned (I had it before) to question why I have to go through this alone, with no husband to hold me and agree with me that it will be alright. Immediately I began to thank Jesus for being my husband and comforting me. I then had a picture come to my mind. It was Jesus sitting back on a big pillow, and I was laying my head on His chest as he held me tight, hugging me, telling me it was going to be alright. I felt safe and comforted. It seemed very real. I fell asleep with that picture in my mind and heart. If there had been any doubt that I would be okay, this vision took care of it!

I went into surgery the next morning with great peace and the joy of knowing I was going to come out better in many ways! When I woke up from surgery later that day I the doctors told me this cancer had become aggressive; it had completely blocked one of the two large arteries going into the lung and had invaded the second. It had also invaded some lymph nodes in the lung. Because of these things it could not be repaired, and they had to remove the entire lung.

Just over four months later I wrote a letter to my pastor about my experience. I wrote, "I can tell you that I am much better, much stronger physically and spiritually than I was before the surgery." I can't say it has been easy. Recovery and building strength takes time. It is a process.

Although it was quite difficult at first, I made the effort several times a day during the weeks of recovery to walk through my house reading healing and other encouraging scriptures to myself. As I was strong enough, I read some out loud. With every discouraging thought that tried to come I counteracted it with scripture. I kept healing scriptures, as well as books and CDs on healing out and ready to use at all times. I did use them often.

Now, let me clarify something. I did not obsess with trying to do nothing but read scriptures and pray. I let my body and mind recuperate. I rested, I slept, I watched funny TV shows and favourite movies. I talked with friends. Each day, even in the middle of the night when I could not sleep I would pull out my list of scriptures, or a book, or plug in a CD of healing scriptures. I used the word as a weapon and as a comfort.

About a week before I was released to go back to work I felt a heaviness in my soul, a depression that attempted to come to me. I realized that in the natural process of healing after a surgery this will sometimes happen, but I also knew this was a spiritual thing. So I took authority over it in the name of Jesus. I proclaimed my deliverance from any demonic oppression or depression and declared, "By the work of Jesus Christ I am free from those things, and they cannot work against me!" I commanded it to leave in the name of Jesus.

In my mind, I envisioned demons of depression and infirmity standing throughout my house. I did not try to imagine this, but the pictures just came to my mind. I knew this was a vision from God showing me in the spirit what was happening. These demons had come to take advantage of me while I was physically down. In my mind, the word that I was speaking in Jesus' name appeared as a sword swinging at the demons, driving them out of my house as they ran in terror. The cloud began lifting and within just a few days my positive outlook was back. The sun was shining in my heart again, and I felt bright hope for my future with no gray shades in my life.

All through the summer my friends and I had been praying that God would continue to direct the doctors involved with my case. I was to see the oncologist for the first time on September 5 to determine if I needed chemotherapy or radiation. So we prayed that he would not recommend anything I did not truly need and that he would not miss anything that needed to be treated.

The entire month of September I was in limbo waiting for the oncologist and the Tumor Board to review various tests they had performed on me. The carcinoma they had removed from my lung was stage III. According to my oncologist, the new cancer treatment guidelines indicated chemo would be needed. However, he wanted to be sure that was really necessary because I was doing so well (he told me this). He wanted to review the tests they did on the lung they had removed and determine if every part was coded right for determining the diagnosis level and off course he wanted other tests as well. I knew our prayers were being answered that he was taking extra care in determining if chemo was needed or not. I have heard so many people say that their oncologist immediately sent them to chemo, and if they refused to have it, the doctor would drop them. So I knew this doctor was exercising caution on my behalf, which was an answer to our prayers.

I was declared free of cancer on October 1st of 2012 by the oncologists, and he released me. Of course, this was just a confirmation of what I already knew in my spirit. As soon as he said "You need no further treatment, all tests show you are cancer free" I said, "I

KNEW IT!" His Physician Assistant was standing next to me and blurted out, "I KNEW you KNEW it!" The doctor patted my shoulder, with a coy smile and said, "I hope never to have to see you again." I walked out of the oncologist's office that day with the answer to my prayers, knowing I would not have to endure chemo or radiation.

Over the course of the summer, I was off work for seven weeks, on Family/Medical Leave. There is no pay with FMLA, so I went a full month with no check from my job. However, I received checks, as well as cash and grocery gifts from friends all through my time off. I never had to ask for help, it just showed up at my door! My rent, car, and utilities were all taken care of, and I always had groceries in the house! God is gracious to provide so abundantly. There was even extra money to help make up for the time I had to take off each week in August and part of September for Pulmonary Therapy. My job worked wonderfully with me in more ways than I can say. I was back to full 40-hour weeks by October of 2012 and God is still working wonderfully in my circumstances. I praise Him for his goodness and love to me. Keeping my focus on the Word and what Jesus has provided kept me in peace through this ordeal. His peace allowed me to live happy by living out of His joy in my heart.

I want you to be encouraged, whether healthy or sick, to regularly study healing and faith. Get some good teaching books and highlight healing scriptures in your Bible to confess over yourself and your loved ones. You don't know when you may need this as an active part of your life to get you through something.

Also, don't be afraid to go to a doctor. If you have prayed and believed for your healing, but symptoms persist, allow God to get his healing to you any way He can. He loves you. He wants you healed and well. He is Lord, and He always wants the best for you. Trust Him for the best to come to you in each circumstance. He will work with you. Remember, it brings Him glory when His people are healed and walk in health. So be determined to bring Him glory and to keep your joy! If you do, you will have learned how to truly be happy, no matter what.

One final note I am adding now, three years after surgery. I still speak healing scriptures over myself and read books on God's healing. Each time I have to take a regular medical test I praise God before and during the test that it will prove I am healed! Each scheduled test, including pet scans, continue to show I am cancer free! It is apparent to me now that this disease was another attempt by Satan to take me out of God's plans and purposes for my life, one of which is to publish this book. I will never know, until heaven, just how many people the Holy Spirit has helped through this book to find a deeper relationship with God. How many young ministers will be inspired to greater depths of teaching or how many Christian's sitting in the church pew will be moved into a healing ministry after reading these testimonies?

Chapter 10

Are You On The ROAD TO SALVATION?

If you have not received Jesus as your Saviour, please follow the steps in this article. If you are an active Christian read this and refresh your understanding of the salvation you received.

Do you know for SURE if you are going to Heaven? If you had to convince God why He should let you into heaven, what would you say?

The first and foremost thing for each of us is to be sure we have genuinely believed in Jesus Christ as our Savior and made Him our Lord. You cannot be born into salvation by natural birth. Being good, going to church, or being religious does not make you a believer. The following scriptures show the path to salvation in Jesus Christ. Once you have confessed Him as God's Son, and as your Lord and Savior you are on a path of obedience that can open up the fullness of what God has for your life.

"The Word is near you, in your mouth and in your heart- that is, the word of faith which we are preaching, that if you confess with your mouth Jesus as Lord, and believe in your heart that God raised Him from the dead, you shall be saved; for with the heart man believes, resulting in righteousness, and with the mouth he confesses, resulting in salvation." - Romans 10:8-10

John 1:12 promises, "But as many as received Him, to them He gave the right to become children of God, even to those who believe in His name."

In Acts 16:25-29 Paul and Silas were thrown into prison because of their teaching about Jesus. They spent the night praying and praising God when a miraculous, supernatural earthquake happened breaking open the prison doors and even breaking loose the chains of everyone in the jail. In verse 30 the Philippian Jailer brought Paul and Silas out of their prison cell after the earthquake and asked, "Sirs, what must I do to be saved?" Paul answered in verse 31, "Believe in the Lord Jesus, and you shall be saved, you and your household." You can read in verses 32-34 that he and his whole family were joyfully saved that night.

God assures us in Acts 10:34, 35 that He does not show partiality in His gift of Salvation. If he accepted the Philippian jailer and his family, He would accept anyone who calls on Him. Perhaps you are now thinking, "Okay, I know I have salvation, but what now?"

Once we are saved, we have the responsibility to get to know God through His word and prayer. As we read and study the Bible, our mind will continually be renewed, and we will grow in our relationship with Christ. Spiritual growth and maturity are expected to come, but we must do our part to learn what pleases God and in doing so our love for Him grows. When we are in love with Jesus, it becomes a joy to make choices in life that will please God.

Do you believe that you can make God smile and bring joy to His heart? We all have that ability if we choose to do so. None of us is perfect, except Jesus. So we all have weaknesses and mess up a lot. That is not what determines if we love Him. It is what we do with our weaknesses and mess ups that reveal if we are "in love" with Him or not. When we suspect that we are not, we can simply start over, right there. Repent and start anew. That is God's grace! He has already redeemed you if you want that redemption to be yours, but it is up to you to accept it and take that redemption for yourself. He offers it to you. It comes through His Son Jesus.

It is completely your choice whether to receive redemption from the ravages of sin and be a part of God's kingdom. The choice is also yours whether you will live in peace, health, and harmony after you receive His salvation. It is your choice. Rest assured, if you do not choose by your thoughts, words, and actions it will not *just* happen. Choose life, eternal life! Put your trust in Jesus.

A Salvation Confession...

Dear Jesus, I believe you are God's Son. Thank you for taking ALL my sins from the past, present and the future. You have paid the price for my sins. You have delivered me from the curse of sin, which is poverty, sickness, and spiritual death. I now accept what you have done for me, dear Jesus. I repent of all my sins. I ask You to come into my heart and be my Lord. I forgive those who have sinned against me. I ask You to bless them. Help them come to know You better. I receive the forgiveness You offer. I thank You that You have destroyed the power of sin by Your precious blood. Thank You that you have cleansed me in Your blood and continually cleanse me each day from everything not in conformity to Your will in purpose, thought and action. I rely on You for it. Thank You, Jesus, for being my Savior. Thank You for Your Holy Word, the Bible. I will commit myself to reading it and learning more about You and Your plan for my life. I ask you now to fill me with Your Holy Spirit so I can know you better.

(Scripture References: Isaiah 53:4-6; Galatians 3:13-14; Colossians 1:13-14; I John 1:9; Romans 10:9-11; Acts 1:8; Acts 2:38-39)

Made in the USA
Lexington, KY
16 September 2015